THE NEUROTIC NOTEBOOK

THE NEUROTIC NOTEBOOK

Lena Friedrich

Andrews McMeel
PUBLISHING®

Dedicated to those who prefer to think on paper.

I've
been
margi-
nalized.

I don't make a good impression.

t's hard

to fit in

) I'm an outsider (

No one notices me.

I just don't measure up.

I'm a total Ⓕailure.

e
s
s
.

I
feel
spine

I wish I was **bold**.

INT. - NIGHT

                    ME
          I feel like I am
          always acting.

❏ I seek approval from others.

Do y u think I lack character?

I feel the
need   to
justify
myself.

I'm the shadow of my former self.

I was meant to rule,
not to be ruled.

- I thought I was bulletproof.

~~I've been double-crossed.~~

My words were distorted.

i've lost my capital.

I'm

in a

really

bad

spot

right now.

```
     I  |  feel          \  broken down.
     S  |   V          \  totally      Adv
                        Adv
```

I | feel \ broken down.
S | V Adv

totally
Adv

I'm <u>stressed</u> out.

I feel oppressed by my background.

Ineedsomespace.

I want to get off the grid.

I need a change in landscape.

Help me break away!

I'm bleeding.

I'm bleeding.

I might've contracted something.

I need to pull myself together.

can

my

How

I

find

center?

I am looking for guidance.

1:00

11:00

8:00

3:00

6:00

2:00

12:00

4:00

5:00

9:00

7:00

10:00

8:00

4:00

2:00

12:00

5:00

6:00

I'm not much of a planner.

11:00

7:00

10:00

6:00

9:00

1:00

8:00

3:00

I'm a dreamer.

I can't keep my resolution.

No matter how hard I try,
I never finish anyth

I just feel like I'm going around and around in circles. I just feel like I'm going

Nothing fulfills me.

I accentuate the négative.

I'm on edge.

I am going through a tr

ansition.

I am prematurely graying.

I'M HAVING A MIDPAGE CRISIS.

~~I am in complete denial.~~

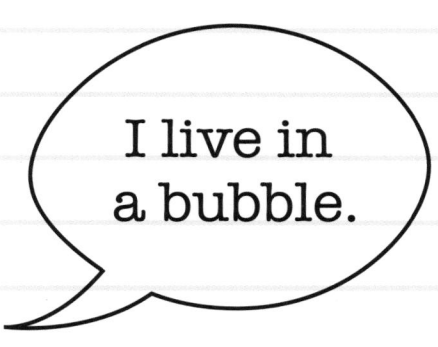

It feels gre

to   open   up   .

I'm sick of being put in a box.

I'm not just a number.

People read me the wrong way.

Look beneath the surface.

There are so many layers to me..

I \ˈī, ə\ *pron* : can't be defined

I have a split personality disorder.

I don't have a split personality disorde

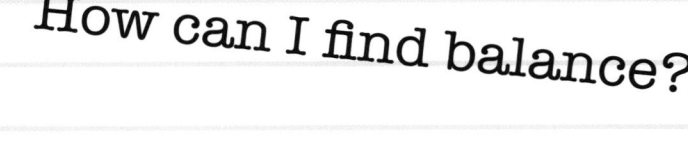

How can I find balance?

I feel so dis-
connected.

"I don't sound like myself."

I

HAVE

COMPLETELY

LOST SIGHT OF

WHO I AM AND

WHAT IS REALLY IMPORTANT TO ME

I hope things will turn around.

I know I'm in good hands.

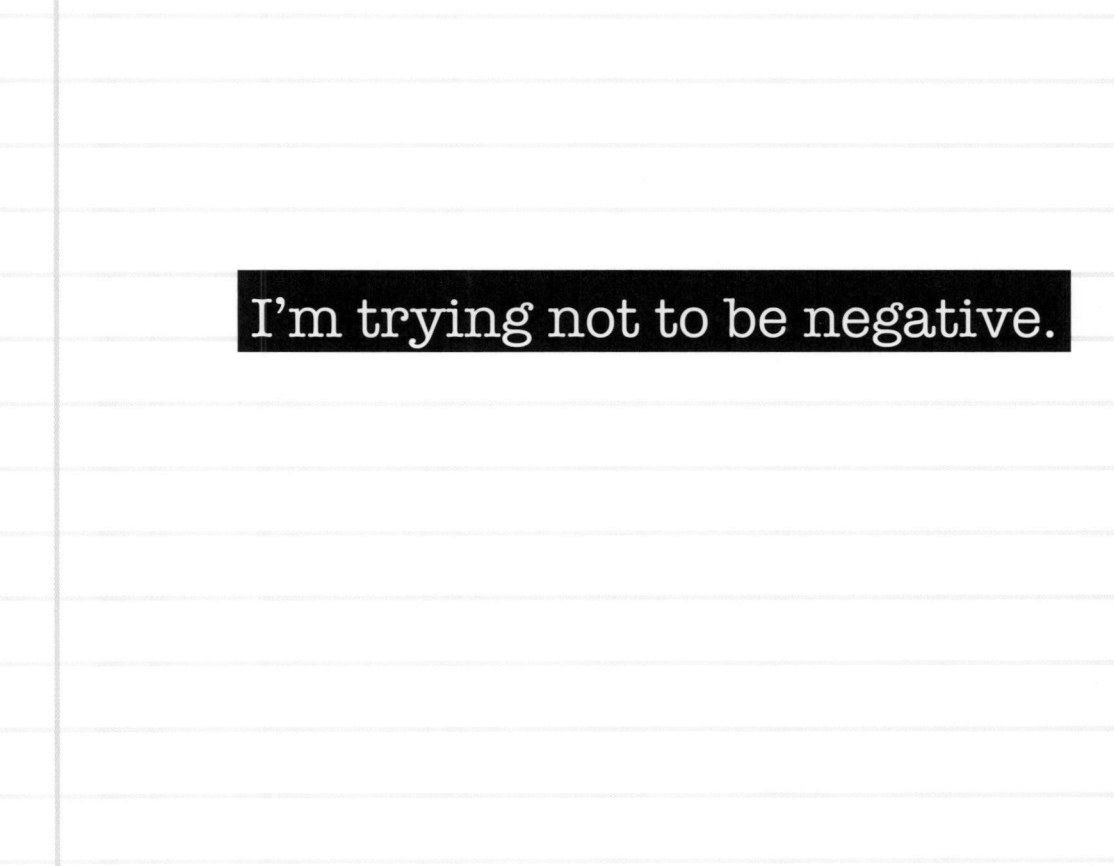

I'm trying not to be negative.

{I need to brace myself.}

I can stop these recurring thoughts. I can
stop these recurring thoughts. I can sto
these recurring thoughts. I can stop the
curring thoughts. I can stop these recur
thoughts. I can stop these recurring tho
I can stop these recurring thoughts. I ca
stop these recurring thoughts. I can sto
these recurring thoughts. I can stop the
curring thoughts. I can stop these recur
thoughts. I can stop these recurring tho
I can stop these recurring thoughts. I ca
stop these recurring thoughts. I can sto
these recurring thoughts. I can stop the
curring thoughts. I can stop these recur
thoughts. I can stop these recurring tho
I can stop these recurring thoughts. I ca
stop these recurring thoughts. I can sto
these recurring thoughts. I can stop the
curring thoughts. I can't stop these recu
ring thoughts. I can stop these recurrin
thoughts. I can stop these recurring tho
I can stop these recurring thoughts. I ca
stop these recurring thoughts. I can sto
these recurring thoughts. I can stop the

thoughts. I can stop these recurring thoug.
I can stop these recurring thoughts. I can
stop these recurring thoughts. I can stop
these recurring thoughts. I can stop these
curring thoughts. I can stop these recurrir
thoughts. I can stop these recurring thoug.
I can stop these recurring thoughts. I can s
these recurring thoughts. I can stop these
curring thoughts. I can stop these recurrir
thoughts. I can stop these recurring thoug.
I can stop these recurring thoughts. I can s
these recurring thoughts. I can stop these
curring thoughts. I can stop these recurrir
thoughts. I can stop these recurring thoug.
I can stop these recurring thoughts. I can s
these recurring thoughts. I can stop these
curring thoughts. I can stop these recurrir
thoughts. I can stop these recurring thoug.
I can't stop these recurring thoughts. I car
stop these recurring thoughts. I can stop
these recurring thoughts. I can stop these
curring thoughts. I can stop these recurrir
thoughts. I can stop these recurring thoug.
I can stop these recurring thoughts. I can s

I just need to decompress.

I could really use a date.

__ / __ / ____

I'm begging for attention.

I'm looking for my better half

Read between the lines.

I think I am getting attached.

thereisatruelinkbetween.us

You bring color to my life.

I don't feel so empty anymore.

Y__ C_MP_ET_ M_.

I'

b

u

d

t

b

w

t

y

u

m

o

n

o

e

i

h

o

Do you do analog?

. I guess I crossed the line.

Do you want a piece of me?

Do you want a piece of me?

Do you want a piece of me?

Do you want a piece of me?

Do you want a piece of me?

Do you want a piece of me?

Do you want a piece of me?

Do you want a piece of me?

Do you want a piece of me?

I   at a loss   words...

I thought we were on the same

page.

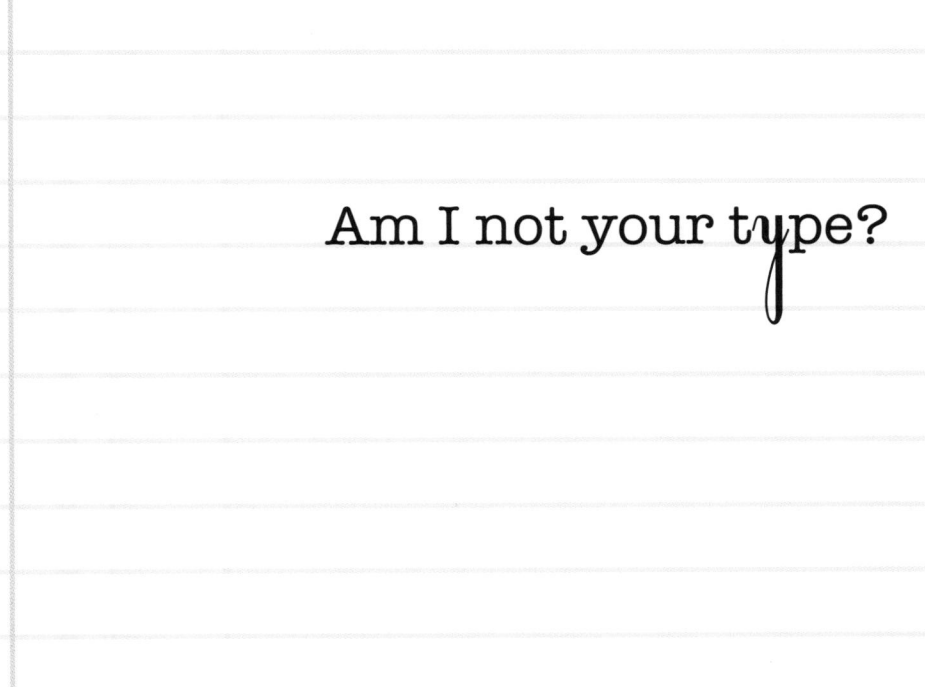

Am I not your type?

Maybe I'm projecting here.

Is this transference?

I ███
should ███.
███████████ probably █████████████████████████████
███
███ censor ██
███████ myself.
███
███████████████████
████████████
██████

I just can't resist my inclination.

I am narcissistic.

I Feel Entitled

I wsih I could
correct my mistake.

I'd give an arm and a leg
to save our relationship.

I feel much lighter now.

I need a new perspective.

ght   - I have so many options.

densed Light   - I have so many options.

gular   - I have so many options.

densed   - I have so many options.

mibold   **- I have so many options.**

ld   **- I have so many options.**

ndensed Bold   **- I have so many options.**

I'm done being walked all over!

I can protect myself ©

From now on comma
I won't let anyone dictate me period

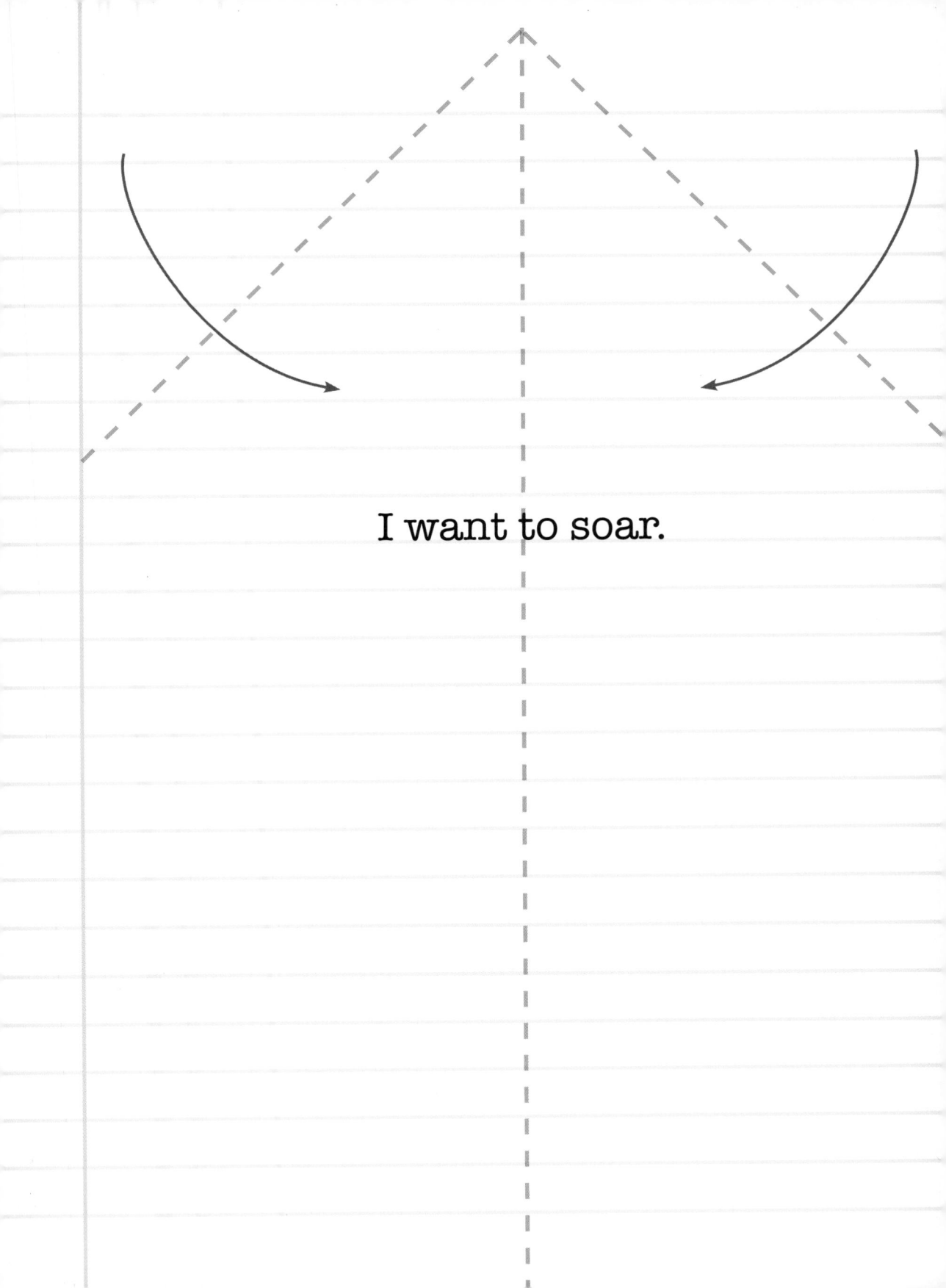

I want to soar.

I can coun on myself.

step.

by

step

take it

need to

I just

There is no short(ctrl + X) to success.

i'lL kEEp dOiNg mY BeSt iN anY caSe.

It will be alright in The End.